iOS 14

USER GUIDE

A Simple Guide To Unlock Hidden Features, With Screen Shot Tricks And Tips Of The New iOS 14 For Dummies And Seniors.

By

Robert A. Young

Table of Contents

iOS 14 1

USER GUIDE.. 1

Copyright © 2020 Robert A. Young 2

CHAPTER ONE 1

iOS 14 REVIEW 1

CHAPTER TWO.................................... 7

iPhones AND iPads THAT SUPPORT iOS14.. 7

CHAPTER THREE 11

HOW TO DOWNLOAD AND INSTALL iOS 14 and iPadOS 14 11

CHAPTER FOUR 13

HOW TO CHANGE APPS ICONS ON NEW iOS 14 HOME SCREEN 13

CHAPTER FIVE.................................. 17

SIRI... 17

CHAPTER SIX 25

MAPS ON iOS 14.............................. 25

CHAPTER SEVEN 33

SAFARI ON iOS14 33

CHAPTER EIGHT............................... 41

APP LIBRARY IN iOS 14......................41

CHAPTER NINE..................................47

CARPLAY...47

CHAPTER TEN....................................51

NEW FEATURES WITH iOS 14...........51

CHAPTER ELEVEN............................. 58

HIDDEN iOS 14 AND iPadOS 14
FEATURES.. 58

CHAPTER ONE

iOS 14 REVIEW

iOS 14 changes the way you organize and use your iPhone for the better. But third parties will need to accept things like widgets and shop videos in this update.

At present

The widget may appear on the home screen, better navigation with the library app

Maps and messages receive acceptable support

Siri small notification files, telephones

Against it

Third-party widgets and applications require some work

iOS 14 releases the most difficult task of smartphone software analysis. An update that introduces a lot of changes - and this has been the most important feature of iOS for a while - iOS 14 does not feel like you've entered a volatile room in your home after someone repaired furniture. Things revolve around iOS 14, but seriously, you do it all.

With iOS 14, Apple is introducing an updated way to rotate your iPhone. Instead of scrolling from page to page, the new application library is ready for everything in the folders, making it easier to navigate to the applications we want. Widgets have been released for invisibility on this modern screen and can now live on your home screen. Even if the video is no longer wall-mounted, a feature such as picture-by-picture allows you to watch the video while working on other applications.

How to download iOS 14?

Instead of the latest version, existing apps like Messages and Maps get points in iOS 14. Many new additions, such as the Converter program, bring acceptable functionality to iOS, although there is still a good performance balance.

When the developer beta dropped in the summer I started using iOS 14 again and I continued to do so with a full update to be released in September. My trial of iOS 14 has received software updates that are a big step forward for Apple phones, however, many features will be unlocked when developers have the opportunity to use these new features.

IOS 14 Test: Compatibility

IOS 14 is available for free without any condition. To download iOS 14, go to App Settings on your iPhone and select General and Software Updates. Then you can follow the on-screen instructions on how to install the update.

You need an iPhone 6s or later to use iOS 14. You can still run the latest version of Apple software. The new software will be pre-installed on the iPhone 12 when new models are launched next month.

In my review of iOS 14, I tested the software updates on the original iPhone SE and the new iPhone 11 Pro Max. I've seen my iPhone SE's battery life tapping but shouldn't have a problem activating the old phone update.

IOS 14 Test: Widget

Without forcing you to start using, the widget gives you clear information about the type of data you need - think about current temperatures, upcoming meetings, or more recent headlines and sports articles. As of today, the widget is on the screen today, forcing you to scroll up to the home screen. IOS 14 saves you trouble by allowing you to place widgets on your home screen between your apps.

IOS 14 Test (Image Case: Tom's Guide)

Even better, Apple offers many of the same widget options, which look richer and in some cases more informative than they did on iOS 13. The new weather widget, for example, could be a simple square indicating the current temperature, a rectangular box with long extended weather, or a very large block estimating the estimated hours. The size of the widget you choose depends on you.

I set up my home screen to set up a weather widget among my favorite apps to see the temperature of my current location. At various points in my experiment, I had no screen other than a widget - one dedicated to topics from

Apple's news app, one showing me what's next on my TV line, and finally a stack of photos, calendars, and other built-in apps. . (A little more about Smart Stack.)

You have many ways to add widgets. You can click on the screen today until the option appears on the home screen before dragging the widget to where you want it.

CHAPTER TWO

iPhones AND iPads

THAT SUPPORT iOS14

iPhones

Apple has officially launched iOS 14 with a widgeted home screen, email and browser configuration capability, and much more. Does your iPhone support iOS 14? Go below for a complete list of compatible devices.

Apple claims that iOS 14 can run on iPhone 6s and later on iOS 13. It is exactly iOS 13. This means that any iPhone that supports iOS 13 will also support iOS 14. Here is a complete list of iPhone models and iPods. Powered by iOS 14:

- 11th telephone
- iPhone 11 Pro
- iPhone 11 Pro Max
- iPhone XS
- iPhone XS Max
- XR phone
- X Phone
- 8th Phone
- iPhone 8 Plus
- iPhone 7
- iPhone 7 Plus
- iPhone 6s
- iPhone 6S Plus
- iPhone SE (first generation)
- iPhone SE (2nd generation)

- iPod Touch (7th Generation)

Support for the iPhone SE and iPhone 6s is amazing. People are convinced that iOS 13 will continue to support devices and is now expanding to iOS 14. iPhone SE and iPhone 6s users can install and run on their devices iOS 14.

Updates include home screen widget support, the power of the new Apple Maps, the image support image, and much more.

iPad that support iOS14

Most iPads will upgrade to the iPad 14. Apple has confirmed that the iPad Air 2 and later will be available on all iPad Pro models, the iPad 5th generation, and later the iPad Mini 4 and later.

Here is a complete list that will support iPadOS 14 devices:

- iPad Air 2 (2014)
- iPad Air (2019)
- iPad mini 4 (2015)
- iPad Mini (2019)
- iPad (2017, 2018, 2019)
- iPad Pro 9.7in (2016)
- iPad Pro 10.5in (2017)
- iPad Pro 11in (2018, 2020)
- iPad Pro 12.9in (2015, 2017, 2018, 2020)

CHAPTER THREE

HOW TO DOWNLOAD AND INSTALL iOS 14 and iPadOS 14

Apple's new software updates for the iPhone and iPad, iOS 14 and iPadOS14 are set to launch and bring a host of new features. In iOS 14, you can add widgets to your home screen, watch videos in the wizard, and use the new Apple Active Speech app. In iPadOS 14, you can manually type text boxes and use the customized search experience. Both software updates provide maps, messaging, Safari, and Siri enhancements.

Here's what you need to know to download and install new updates.

Open the Settings app on your device and click "Normal"

Then click "Software Update"

You will want to see an ad describing the update. (If you do not see the notification, try again later.) Click on the "Download and Install" option and follow the instructions from there. The update is already downloaded to your device - in that case, you will need to click "Install" to continue the process.

Please note that while installing the update, you will never be able to use your device. It may take some time to install the updates - in my experience, 15 minutes or more - for this reason, I may wait until the evening to install the update overnight.

CHAPTER FOUR

HOW TO CHANGE APPS ICONS ON NEW iOS 14 HOME SCREEN

Allows you to freely customize the look of your home screen by changing the automatic icons and images you choose. Before you follow this guide, you will need to find or create an image of your home software icon, and much more to download online.

The following steps explain how to add a custom icon to the home screen of any app you like.

Touch the app icons by installing the shortcut first, then the app

If you find it problematic to remove and run shortcuts to the app every time you open an app with a custom icon, do or should not use only shortcuts that you can use regularly.

Shortcuts can be a modern tool to use because it allows users to create different programs that work on their devices, but in this case, shortcuts include only one basic element.

Launch shortcuts on your iPhone or iPad.

Select the icon in the upper right corner of the device screen.

Tap the add-on.

Use the text field to browse the open application.

Select Open Application.

Select Select.

Use the browse application to change the icon and select it.

Tap the three dots that is in the upper right corner of your device.

Press Application Holder.

From the drop-down menu, select the photo, or select the file, depending on where the application image appears.

Select an image to change.

In the text field, rename the application as needed to appear on the home screen.

Tap Add.

Tap. Your shortcut is already done.

Return to the home screen.

If you already have apps on your home screen, you now have two features. To save your newly created icon, move the old icon to the library. You do not need to disable the original application.

This process is time-consuming, especially when it comes to finding or

creating custom icons that you will not
need to do in every application.

CHAPTER FIVE

SIRI

Siri status change for iOS 14 is its enhanced visibility. Instead of taking full screen, Siri now only uses a small portion of your iPhone display, allowing you to view the apps you are currently using.

While there has been some attention to the changes in the network, there are still some things in Siri in a recent announcement.

This guide explains how to use new questions and activities.

You Can Send Audio Messages On Siri With The Updated iOS 14

Call Siri by clicking a button or by the "Siri Siri" command.

Say "Send listening message".

When prompted, enter the name of the contact to which the message will be sent.

When the "Okay, recording" message appears, start the audio recording.

When you have finished recording, stop talking or keep quiet for a few seconds.

When the first message appears, you will be asked if you want to send it. Say "yes" to send immediately without looking, or click send.

Alternatively, say "No" or click Cancel to not send the message.

You can view the message by clicking the button next to Recording in the compact box at the top of the screen.

What you see when recording a video message with the Siri app in iOS 14

If you do not want to record a message, you can add pre-recording questions like "Hey Siri, send an audio message to Felix".

Get Bicycle Guide From Siri In iOS 14

Call Siri and ask me "Find a bike for me at home" or a similar question. In contrast, "I've found a bike path from place to place" provides a way between two things.

Once Apple Maps is open, click the path you want to take.

share estimated arrival time using Siri in iOS 14

Open Apple Maps and navigate to Siri and say "Share my ETA".

Provide the name of the contact or contacts to send the message when requested.

In the initial attempt to do so, you will need to accept the privacy statement stating that your name and email address on your Apple ID should be shared. Confirm with Siri by saying "yes".

Shared ETA is only available when used to browse Apple maps, so make sure it provides guidance before attempting to share.

How has Siri translation improved?

Apple has incorporated the new translation app into real-time translation, which also provides limited

Siri conversion for many years. Ready for 2020 with a slight change.

First, Apple revised the neural writing-speaking wording to work beyond U.S. English, including a number of English writings. This helps to give Siri a more natural feel in the translations as well as in the general story.

Languages that support Siri native language in iOS 14?

- English (Australia, India, Ireland, South Africa, United Kingdom, United States)
- French
- German
- Japanese
- Mandarin Chinese
- Spanish (Spain, Mexico)

Apple has improved the ability to translate Siri and now it is available in 65 languages.

Languages Siri Translate

- Arabic
- French
- German
- Italian
- Japanese
- Mandarin Chinese
- Portuguese
- Russian
- Spanish
- English (United States) to Korean.
- From Arabic (United Arab Emirates, Saudi Arabia) to English.
- French to English, German, Italian, Mandarin Chinese, Portuguese, Russian, Spanish.
- German to English, French, Italian, Mandarin Chinese, Portuguese, Russian, Spa Spanish.
- Italian can also be translated to, French, Chinese, Portuguese,

Mandarin English Russian, Spanish, and German.

- Japanese is English, Mandarin Chinese, Korean.
- Korean to English, Japanese, Mandarin Chinese.
- From Mandarin Chinese (Mainland China) to English, French, German, Italian, Japanese, Korean, Spanish too.
- Mandarin Chinese (Taiwan) to English, Japanese.
- Portuguese (Brazil) to English, French, Italian, Spanish, Russian.
- Russian to English, French, Italian, Portuguese, Russian, Spanish.
- Spanish to English, French, Italian, Mandarin Chinese, Portuguese, Russian.

How well do you know Siri?

Apple has created a chart of Siri's knowledge, it's basic banking and information about various things.

CHAPTER SIX

MAPS ON iOS 14

With all iOS updates, Apple constantly adds new features to active apps, and iOS 14 is no exception. Most apps have new important features, including Apple Map, which gets a bike guide, EV routes, guides, and more.

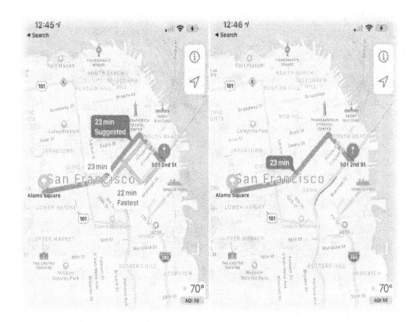

This guide highlights all the new and updated features Apple added to the Maps app in the new iOS and iPadOS 14.

Bicycle guides

Maps on iOS 14 provide cycling directions for first-time cyclists, similar to Google Maps. Bicycle lanes, bike paths, and well-traveled trails are considered to get you where you want to go.

You can preview the height of your route, see how difficult it can be, and see how crowded the streets are. There are ways to avoid long slopes or stairs where your bike should be ridden.

The bike guide extends to Apple Watch on Watch OS 7, with easy navigation and voice guidance, and instructional maps.

Cycling directions are limited to a few cities, including New York, Los Angeles, San Francisco, Beijing, and Shanghai.

Roads with EV stops

If you have an iPhone-compatible electric car, maps automatically add charging points to your system when planning a trip.

The option of the EV route is also responsible for the time taken to make the estimated arrival time, and the use of maps can track current charges and charger types to provide routes designed for electric vehicle owners.

To use this feature you need to synchronize the electric vehicle with the iPhone and it will not work if you are planning a trip with a friend who uses an electric vehicle as it is not an option available without EV.

Currently, EV parking lots work with vehicles from BMW and Ford.

Guidelines

On iOS 13, Apple added "Add-ons" that allows you to create a list of places to visit for yourself and your friends and family. In iOS 14, "extension" is referred to as "guidelines".

You can continue to customize your devices to iOS / iPadOS 14 '(or macOS Big Sur), but Apple has now opted to guide the selection of trusted features.

Provide guidance on the best place to visit in the city, and provide tips on places to eat, shop, and explore. Guides can be saved to maps and updated automatically when new locations are added.

Other Apple partners in the guide include Lonely Planet, Washington Post, Altrails, Infusion, and more.

How to use guides on Apple Maps

Extension of redesign

Apple last year launched a revised map with more details on roads, buildings, parks, beaches, marinas, forests, and more, and updated iOS 14 mapping is expanding into new areas.

Speed cameras

If you have speed cameras and bright red cameras on your way, Apple will now notify you when you reach them. There is an option to see where the cameras are on the map.

Refine location

If you are not using GPS in an urban area and the maps do not register you in the right place, you can use a new upgrade to find the exact location for better reading.

Use your iPhone to scan nearby buildings to minimize your location while picking up an extra item for iOS 13.

Because it uses the surrounding areas, the cleaner is limited to areas including San Francisco, New York, Boston, Chicago, Houston, Las Vegas, Philadelphia, Washington, DC, and Hawaii. Cleaning the area is done by the improved environment.

Combinations

Reduce congestion in areas where traffic is light in large cities, such as Paris and London. IOS 14 maps show compact area prices and provide ways you can use them when you need them.

There are cities where license plates restrict access to certain routes, and Apple Maps now supports license plate information, so you may decide that you will be allowed to use the route one day.

CHAPTER SEVEN

SAFARI ON iOS14

This guide includes all the new features and modifications you can find in Safari 14 for iPhone and iPad.

Improving speed and performance

According to Apple, Safari iOS 14 has a "faster JavaScript engine" which makes Safari 2 times faster than the channel on Android.

Built version

OS 14 has a translation option in Safari, which translates the site into English, Spanish, Chinese, French, German, Russian, or Brazilian Portuguese, and has been added to update Apple's new interpretation program.

Translating a web page is as easy as clicking on the "aA" icon in the menu bar to access a web page in the supported language as well as the translation option. Click Translate, the web page will automatically translate to the language on your phone.

Additional languages that you can translate can be added to the iPhone settings program as shown below.

Safari in OS 14 can track stored passwords by searching for packages related to data breaches.

To illustrate this point, Apple uses Safari printing technology to constantly check your passwords, contrary to a list of passwords that Apple promises as a secure and hidden method. If a breach is encountered, Safari will notify you and, if possible, give you an incentive to update Apple login or to automatically generate a secure password.

You can see the potential issues under the heading "Security Tips" in the password setting section of the app.

Confidentiality Declaration

Adds a report on the growing confidentiality of Safari (and Makos Big Sur) prevention operations in OS 14. Over the past few years, Apple has been working to curb cross-site traffic that uses websites to monitor Internet usage when you search for various websites, targeting advertising, analytics, and more.

Smart Search Blocking is a list of driver blocking tools from Safari by Apple and iOS 14, a list of sites where Apple uses trackers, how many of these sites are installed, and the most common trackers you will find when browsing the web.

Any website that makes money or uses the marketing network for these purposes has these tracks, just like any other website that uses analytics services such as Google Analytics to collect data on website user behavior and content improvement.

Safari on the iPhone and iPad lists the number of browsers per website you visit, the number of blocked users, the number of websites you visit with the browser, and a list of the most common routes that appear to be Google double-click. . Net.

You can access the Privacy Report section of Safari by tapping the icon below and selecting the "Privacy Report" option. Note that you need to stop cross-tracking for the Privacy Statement to take effect, and the Privacy Statement will encourage you to do something if it is not yet open.

The picture in the picture

In Safari on the iPhone, if you watch a video, you can now click the button to view it in window mode, browse another website, or do something else on your iPhone while the video is playing.

How to Start websites by searching

If you type a URL like apple.com when downloading a search interface to the iPhone, you can click the "Go" button to open the website directly without clicking the link in the search results.

Easy access with Apple

Apple has created new tools for developers to transfer existing web accounts to Apple, making it more secure for iPhone, iPad, and Mac users who want to convert existing logins to Apple.

Search permission

In order to provide personalized ads, you must obtain the user's permission for the applications you want to search through apps and websites. Enable the app to search or request not to follow the two settings for the app, but the app corresponds to the privacy statement to keep you updated on the app usage and web browsing habits.

CHAPTER EIGHT

APP LIBRARY IN iOS 14

IOS 14 is now available for installation! Pay a ransom for new useful features. iPhone users can take advantage of new widgets on the home screen, communicate in foreign languages using Apple's Apple, and tell everyone about it with an improved messaging service. But the most interesting change in the Apple operating system is the addition of a library that allows you to navigate through the pages and pages of the apps that were on the iPhone from the beginning.

In this article, we will show you how you can achieve this important adjustment and why you should be happy about it. To see all that Apple has announced regarding upcoming software enhancements, read our extensive guide to new features in iOS 14.

What is the library article in Apple 14?

Until now, every time you install an app on your iPhone, its icon will automatically be saved on the home screen or connected devices. This means that if you want to get the app, you have to scroll through the various pages until you find it. Yes, you can move it to another page or put it in a folder, but it will always be on the home screen.

The application library changes this by creating a separate area where your application icons can be seen. If you have ever used an Android smartphone, you will know this idea as it has been on the Google platform for many years.

These two things are different, in Android, apps are always stored in alphabetical order or sorted from old to new. Apple Library teams work collaboratively according to their denominations and are featured at WWDC 2020, including entertainment, community, the arts, and more recently entertainment.

Get Library on iOS 14

You will find the New Library Applications page to the right of the last page where applications are now placed. So if you currently have a home page and two more pages, the application library will appear when you swipe left on the third page.

The main screen of the library

Before we use the library, it is worth noting that something new to the organization comes with it.

Being in the Apple Price App Library means you never want to see all the other app screens. Then there is a new way to hide them. Tap and hold on any page to enter the jigsaw mode (when all apps are rotating) and then click the dots at the bottom of the screen to get a closer look. Here you will see all the existing pages, there is a logo at the bottom to indicate that they are active.

Touching any page will deactivate it, which means that it will not show up when you swipe pages in the normal way. Once you are happy with the choice, click full, you are ready. If you find that you have missed some pages, you can always go to the jigsaw mode and re-enable them.

How to use the library in iOS 14

On the Program Library page, you will see a folder in Grid that describes the type of application that contains each name. These are not standard folders, however, and Apple needs to sprinkle a little magic to make them more useful.

Each section has three main application features and a college in the lower right corner.

Ways to use the library in the new iOS 14: Folders

The next touch will open a folder in the normal style, but clicking on any large one (the Apple-recognized apps you use regularly) will open the app itself.

There is one exception to this rule, the Tips folder contains great features that you think will be useful to your iPhone at the moment.

How to use the library in iOS 14: Open folders

If you want to quickly follow an application, but do not want to search for folders, clicking the scroll bar at the top of the page will open a list of all the apps installed in alphabetical order. You can now scroll through the search bar.

How do I get the library on my iPhone?

An app library, new widgets, and improved translator and messaging system, and maps are all part of iOS 14. And the good news is that they are now available.

CHAPTER NINE

CARPLAY

Update CarPlay to iOS 14 Update 14CarPlay to iOS 14 Upgrade to 14CarPlay iOS 14

IPhone 6s and later models all get updates on iOS 14.

For CarPlay users, this new release will bring great improvements, and we will provide the details one by one.

First and foremost, there is iPhone support, which can be used as a car key. This new feature was originally used by BMW and allows Apple iPhone owners to unlock and launch their cars with the click of a button.

The car key is kept in the wallet and will notify us the same way you make a payment through Apple Pay. On the iPhone 11, you can double-click the wallet unlock button. Opening the car door is as easy as bringing the iPhone closer to it and you have to put your smartphone in a park or wireless charger while the engine starts.

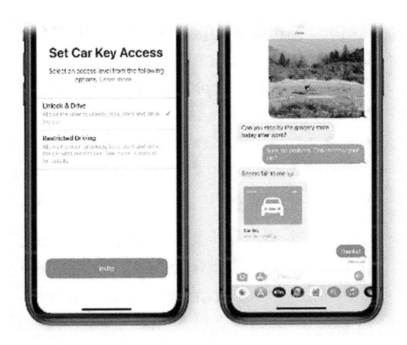

The best part is that you get the full experience from Apple Watch running OSOS 7.

When you set a new car key, users can set full access to the lock, lock, start, and drive, or restrict driving, allowing you to set certain limits. Car keys can be shared between communications using messaging.

The second most important addition to this software update is the support for

Apple Wall wallpapers. Starting with this update, users can go through the settings and select the CarPlay UI Source on their header units. At the moment, Apple does not allow users to set their own photos as wallpapers, so we need to select a list of images first.

CarPlay is the latest blockbuster product from iOS 14. Starting with this release, Car Play can run a wide range of applications, such as parking or charging an electric car. In addition, Apple allows food ordering apps to run on CarPlay, optimized for the driving experience, and without any interruptions.

CHAPTER TEN

NEW FEATURES WITH iOS 14

Key Features and Improvements

Widget

The widget has been redesigned to make it more attractive and data-rich so that it can provide more useful information throughout your day.

Home screen widget

Place the widget anywhere on the home page for information by the view. Perfect for tracking your travels, work, calendar events, or news.

Widgets of different sizes

Widgets now come in small, medium, and large sizes so you can choose the right amount of information.

Widget Gallery

Central to all your widgets from Apple and third parties. The gallery displays high-quality widgets based on multiple installations and users.

Widget channels

You can create up to 10 widgets to get the most out of your home screen. Drag one widget over the other and swipe them.

Smart stack

In the Widget Gallery, you can select Stack Smart, a group of widgets that can be swiped through intelligence tools to get the right widget at the right time based on factors such as time, location, and activity. For example, you can view the Apple News widget in the morning, the events of the day, and the time around the Apple Maps evening.

Siri Suggestions Widget

Siri Suggestions Widget uses an intelligent tool to show you what you can do based on your patterns, such as ordering coffee or starting a podcast. Press the hint to take action without starting the app.

Developer API

Developers can customize their widgets using the new API, allowing them to use updated widgets, including the ability to place them on the home screen and display them in real-time.

Library

Home screen Apple Library

The Apple Library is a new place at the end of your home screen page that automatically transforms all your apps into a simple, easy-to-move feature.

Splits automatically

All the apps on your iPhone are automatically categorized by categories such as Welfare, Production, and Entertainment. Sections are organized intelligently based on application usage.

Tips

The Apple Library shows you recommended apps that you can search for my time, place, or activity.

Check

Use the scroll bar at the top of the app to quickly find the app you are looking for. If you click on the Search option, apps will be displayed alphabetically, making it very easy to scroll through and find what is inside.

Hide original screen pages

You can hide pages to move your home screen, making it easier to access the application library. New apps released from the Apple Store automatically go into the app library

Recently added

You can easily find newly introduced app clips and apps downloaded from the App Store.

Compact UI

Calls

When you receive a call, it looks like a banner instead of a full screen, so you will not be distracted by what you do. Swipe to flush the banner or swipe down to receive additional calls and click Reply.

Third-party VoIP calls

Developer APIs are available for applications such as Skype to support incoming calls.

Face Time Phones

When you receive a FaceTime call, it looks like a banner instead of a full screen. Swipe to disperse the banner or swipe down to access extended FaceTime features.

Siri disk

Siri has a new integrated design that allows you to target information on the screen and introduce your next project without interruption. When you start the app, Siri appears at the bottom of the screen. When Siri affects you, it appears at the top of the screen as a notification. The results have been updated to provide only the information you need for the new composite structure.

The picture in the picture

You can now continue watching the video, or make a face-to-face call while using another app. Make a video call with a friend when you have time to watch or host a TV show while watching your email.

Refresh the image in the image window

You can resize the photo gallery by clicking on the video to enlarge or zoom in.

Move the image to image windows in any corner

Place a video window in any corner of the screen.

CHAPTER ELEVEN

HIDDEN iOS 14 AND

iPadOS 14 FEATURES

The new Apple 14 update for your iPhone and iPad 14 adds $ 699 ($ 699 on Amazon) and the iPad ($ 285 in the marketplace), home screen widgets, an app drawer, and a lot of secret enhancements. . After setting up your phone or tablet you can now install iOS 14 and iPad 14.

This recognition upgrade will definitely enrich your experience, but my favorite strategies for iOS 14 and iPadOS 14 are the ones you need to work on to get them. For example, you can now completely dissolve Apple Mail and Safari with the default app settings.

Getting more like this

Subscribe to Apple's Apple Report and see relevant stories on CNET.

Add your email

Yes, I want to get the CNET Internal Handout, which makes me aware of all the CNET stuff.

I signed up!

By signing up, you agree to the CBS Terms of Use and accept the Data System of our Privacy Policy. You can resign at any time.

Set up your default email or web browser

Apple will eventually give you control over your default apps. Currently, the article is limited to working email and web browsers. For example, Chrome may assign logs to your browser or Outlook as the email of your choice.

App developers need to update their iOS 14 apps and a new default option will appear, you have to be patient if your favorite app is not ready for you.

To get started, open an iPhone or iPad app and scroll down to a list of all your installed apps. Find the email or browser app you want and click on it. If it's updated to iOS 14, you'll see the default app in the browser or Apple's default email; Click on it and select the app you like.

Default app-ios-14

Of course, you can set some default apps in iOS 14.

Quickly remove home application screens

The new iOS 14 library acts as an app drawer, allowing you to remove a few home screens that are rarely full of apps if you've ever used them.

Hide The Original Screen Panel

Do the following:

Tap on the blank area of your home screen to start editing mode. Then, click on the page index, click the checkmark at the bottom of each panel you want to delete. This will not deactivate apps, but will instead take them to the app library, where they are more or less hidden in an app drawer that you can access at any time.

Home screen-ios-14

You can now customize the home screen of your iPhone.

Close the downloaded app on your home screen

You spend that time updating your home screen, adding widgets, and saving your most important apps, only if all your hard work has been ruined by the new program you downloaded. Instead of letting them install your iPhone on your home screen when you install them, send them directly to the Apple Library until they show that they are ready for it.

Open Settings> Home screen and select Library only at the top. You can easily find downloaded apps from the previous user library category, which should be in the top right folder when viewed.

See emoji keyboard

Finally - yes, this is "the end!" You can find emoji selection for what you want. Launch the emoji keyboard as you normally would, and you will now get a scroll bar at the top of the keyboard.

Hidden-photos

Your hidden photo album can now be hidden.

Hidden photos are now hidden

The ability to hide specific photos or videos has been around for a while now on iOS and iPadOS, but there's a big problem - these photos you don't want to see are stored in an album hidden in a remote photo program.